TIME FOR
CHANGE

TIME FOR CHANGE

WHY DO COMPANIES ALWAYS
STRUGGLE WITH SALES?

Dan Harsh

authorHOUSE®

AuthorHouse™
1663 Liberty Drive
Bloomington, IN 47403
www.authorhouse.com
Phone: 1-800-839-8640

Published by AuthorHouse   12/12/2012

ISBN: 978-1-4772-9774-2 (sc)
ISBN: 978-1-4772-9773-5 (e)

Library of Congress Control Number: 2012923195

CONTENTS

INTRODUCTION

This book addresses the hard facts about your Sales organization. You will be confronted with real truths that you have been ignoring. You will be challenged to look at Sales differently than you ever have before.

I want to first point out that the term *Sales* is capitalized throughout this book. I have done this because I feel it deserves it. Sales drives everything.

I have spent the past twenty-five years of my career in Sales. During this time, I have held the positions of inside Sales, outside Sales, Sales manager, vice president of Sales, and owner of two companies. Regardless of my position or the company in which I was employed, striving for more Sales was always the concern and focus.

Why do companies always struggle to generate Sales? Sales is the heartbeat of their company; why haven't they figured out how to make it work? They have learned to run their accounting departments. Employees in accounting don't come in to work and wonder what they are going to do each day. Their operations staff doesn't come in and not have clear direction on what they have to do each day. However, no one provides clear direction for Sales. It doesn't make sense.

Managing Sales is like parenting; everyone does it different. As a result, some Sales organizations grow up to be productive, and some don't grow up—they may simply go out of business. Parenting requires some key elements that have to take place to successfully raise a child. Managing Sales is no different. You have to be willing to make the tough decisions. You must provide direction. You must set the example. You have to provide discipline when necessary. Most of all, Sales, like parenting, is a marathon, not a sprint. You cannot turn Sales on and off or run hard one week and relax the next. It requires a consistent, steady, disciplined, and strategic effort and approach.

Raising a child doesn't just happen on its own. It requires a lot of work, a lot of sleepless nights, and a lot of ups and downs. However, when you're committed to the end result, it makes it a little easier. Sales is a commitment. It requires dedication and a relentless perseverance. For the sake of your company, I am not sure what could possibly be more important.

This book is written to unveil the real truth about Sales. Its purpose is to challenge you to rethink your Sales structure and approach. I will present to you some very specific things to consider. I will share ideas, prompt questions, and provide personal experiences that will help you reevaluate your own situation. I will present to you a definition of Sales that I hope will help you begin to develop a Sales structure that is appropriate for your organization.

My philosophy is built on a Concept, Process, and Discipline. This book will focus on the Concept. I believe when you are done reading this book, you will look at Sales differently than you ever have before. I'm not going to present rocket-science ideas. Rather, what I am presenting is Sales 101. Understanding what I am about to share is fairly easy; implementing it requires a little more effort and definitely more commitment. But most of all, managing and executing it is the real test.

Enjoy.

ACKNOWLEDGMENTS

I could not have attempted to write this book without the help and hard work of many people that surround me. I have been blessed to be associated with individuals that at times make my job very easy. I have probably learned from them much more than they have learned from me.

At the top of the list is my beautiful wife, Valerie. Without her, Concept Services would not exist. I spent many nights lying in bed talking out loud about starting my own company. I would create spreadsheet after spreadsheet of different "what-if" scenarios as I analyzed the risks and rewards. Val would patiently and unselfishly lie there and listen to me each and every night. She would allow me to show her my spreadsheets and explain to her all the detail. Although much of it may not have been very exciting to her, she always gave me her full attention. Then, one night she said, "Dan, just do it. You will not be content until you try it." To this day, I think Nike got their phrase "Just Do It" from Val.

Val went out on a limb when she said "just do it." We had three young children at the time. She was fully aware of the risk and hardship that could and would come on our family. She was willing to sacrifice to allow me the opportunity to achieve a dream. For that I will be eternally grateful for her. She put up with several years of me working sixty-plus hours per week. She has been by my side since the beginning and has never waivered. Val has been active and instrumental in our success from the beginning. She is the chief financial officer of our company and manages the financial side of our organization extremely well.

The real shot in the arm for Concept Services came shortly after my brother Greg joined as a partner in May 2003. Greg joined as the

VP of Sales sixteen months after I formed the company. Greg is the best Sales person I have ever been associated with. He works according to some very basic ideals. He is diligent, never quits, and is full of tenacity. Greg was instrumental in helping identify and form much of Concept Services' foundation. His work ethic, processes and discipline are at the core of our services. Greg's efforts quickly began to have an impact and we had record Sales for six straight years. Some people say you should never go into business with a family member. I can honestly say Greg is the only person I would be comfortable going into business with. Greg's ideas and constant desire to achieve provides ongoing energy for me and those around him.

In our early years, as we were doubling Sales each and every year, I was extremely fortunate to have Becky DeRosa on my staff. I met Becky when Concept Services was only five months old. When I interviewed Becky, I had nothing to offer her except a thirty-day contract. I told her I could not promise her anything beyond thirty days. To this day, I still never understood what compelled Becky to come and work with me. I couldn't offer her full-time employment, I couldn't offer her benefits, I couldn't offer her commission. I couldn't offer her anything beyond thirty days.

It quickly became evident that Becky had talents that I needed to help me manage, operate and grow a young, aggressive organization. Becky provided much of our early discipline. Becky was able to multi-task like I have never seen. I kept giving her tasks and responsibilities and she kept accepting and getting them done. Everything we did was brand-new, needed to be developed for the first time, and Becky was always up for the task. Becky ended up becoming our first manager and was responsible for all day-to-day operations and all of our BDMs (Business Development Reps). Becky brought an energy level to the office unlike anything I have ever experienced. Each day, she was positive and energetic. Her presence caused those around her to work at a higher level. Becky provided the necessary skills, work ethic, and discipline we needed as a young growing company.

In March 2003 I interviewed Traci Whetzel, a young, extremely bright and talented twenty-three-year-old girl. Traci joined Concept Services as a BDM. Traci quickly excelled on every account we threw her way. We began to find other areas in which to utilize Traci's skill sets. Through the years, Traci held multiple positions inside our organization. Often we created new positions to simply watch Traci evolve it to something much more. Traci is a doer. She loved a challenge and always completed things to perfection. Today Traci is our General Manager. She was instrumental in helping us design and implement our training program, our CRM solution and all processes we use. Traci has taken on a great deal of responsibility and works as if she owns Concept Services. Traci has been extremely dependable, which has allowed me to continue to give tasks to her while I focus on other aspects of the company. Traci has been instrumental in raising the achievement bar and the quality of our service to our customers. She demands performance and does not allow quality to take a backseat. I place full trust in Traci, and she has never let me down.

My true success is attributed to those mentioned above. Without them, Concept Services would not exist, and I would not have learned all that I have learned. And lastly, I would not have the opportunity to write this book.

I am extremely blessed to have been surrounded by such quality individuals. I am grateful for all they have done to help me grow as a businessman, but most of all as a person.

CHAPTER 1

DEFINING SALES

What is Sales? If you were to ask this question to ten people, you would get ten different answers. I think that is why many companies struggle with Sales: they haven't defined it for their organization.

Perhaps we would all agree that Sales is the heartbeat of any organization. Then again, maybe we don't all believe that. Maybe that is why companies always struggle with Sales; they don't put that kind of emphasis on it.

I think there can be only one definition of Sales. Having too many definitions or too broad of a definition weakens the entire Sales process and makes it very difficult to achieve your goals. Sales does not need to be complicated or complex. In fact, I think we make it much more difficult than it needs to be. For instance, we throw too many things under the Sales umbrella. We allow Sales to include things that it shouldn't include. As a result, we fool ourselves by believing we are selling when in fact we are simply being busy rather than productive.

We have allowed the term "Sales" to become watered down. When we say Sales, it immediately means so many different things. We have allowed it to lose its focus. Sales needs to be clear, concise and definitive. As a result, I have developed my own definition of Sales.

My definition of Sales is very clear; it is very focused. My definition of Sales leaves no gray area for misinterpretation. Here is my definition of Sales:

"Sales focuses on finding and closing new business
from new customers 100 percent of the time."

1

Read it again.

Anything shy of this should not be considered Sales. Think about it before you respond. I know what you're thinking; I want you to hold your thoughts, as we will address them in a few minutes.

Let's look at this definition closely. First of all, the definition states that Sales focuses on finding new business. We could stop here and talk about this until the cows come home. This is a book by itself. If you stopped the definition right there, it would change everything.

Imagine going to work Monday morning with an understanding that Sales now means "finding new business." You're thinking to yourself that you already consider Sales to mean finding new business. The difference is that now, we are saying it includes *nothing else* but finding new business. Do you have someone in your organization that does nothing but find new business?

Wow, does that make you think differently about Sales? Does that kind of narrow your focus? Does that channel your thoughts and energies? That means during the day when you are taking care of a customer, working on a customer service issue, etc., you are not selling.

Remember the definition: Sales is about finding new business. It's not about customer service issues.

As a Sales manager, if that was what I needed to focus on, that would change everything. How much of your current Sales efforts actually go toward finding new business? Isn't that an interesting question? How much time does your existing Sales force spend trying to find new business? Not how much time they are supposed to, or how much time you think they do, or how much time they say they do. Rather, how much time do they actually spend doing it? I know it is in every account manager's and Sales executive's job description, but how much time do they actually spend doing it?

You already know the answer: very little time is actually spent finding new business. You have known this answer for a long time. And then you wonder why your Sales aren't at the level you would like them to be.

Several studies have determined that only 10 to 20 percent of your Sales reps' time is spent prospecting for new business. My personal experience tells me it is even less than this. If this is true, is it really any wonder that you may not have the level of new business you would like? Is it really any wonder you don't generate the level of Sales you desire?

I remember having a conference call with the Sales reps of one of our customers. The customer was an international freight forwarder. Their Sales reps worked out of their homes and were located throughout the country. During the conversation, we were interrupted with dogs barking in the background and dishes clanging in the sink as they were making food while we talked. I'll share with you later how I feel about working from home.

The Sales reps repeatedly shared how they do not have time to prospect for new business. Their entire day was spent servicing and managing existing customers. They went on to say how competitors are calling on their customers each and every day offering lower pricing and trying to steal them away.

They expressed that in order to maintain these accounts, they were required to work with them every day to keep the competition out. As a result, they did not spend any time prospecting for new business.

The following week, I had a conversation with the VP of Sales of the same organization. This individual was not on the conference call the previous week. During our call he was emphatic about how he needs to close new business. I asked him, "How important is it for you to find new business?" He replied, "It is the number-one priority of my entire Sales force."

How can this be their number-one priority and yet the very thing his Sales force is not doing? How could a Sales manager be so disconnected from his Sales force?

I could share many examples of this very same thing. Do you really know what your Sales reps are doing? Do you really know where they spend their time?

When I meet with customers and prospects, I hear the same thing. Many times, their number-one priority is to find new business. However, when we really look at their Sales force, they all agree that their Sales reps are not spending time in this area. If finding new business from new customers is key and critical to your organization, then why do your Sales reps not spend much of their time doing it?

So let me ask the question again: how much time does your Sales force actually spend prospecting for new business? In most cases, the answer is very little, if any. It doesn't make sense, but it is very true. It is true inside your organization, as well.

Remember, if our definition of Sales is finding new business, and you admit that your Sales reps don't spend much time doing this, then they are not selling according to our new definition.

Let's read my definition of Sales again and take it one step further.

"Sales focuses on finding and closing new business from new customers 100 percent of the time."

Step two says that Sales focuses on finding new business *from new customers.* This changes things a little more. Initially we said that Sales focuses on finding new business. Now we are saying that Sales focuses on finding new business from new customers.

Say it again. *"Sales focuses on finding new business from new customers."*

Imagine showing up for work on Tuesday and the focus of Sales is "finding new business from new customers." Now what? Is your Sales force set up for this? Is this the focus of your Sales reps? Are they equipped to do this? Will they do this? Are you set up to even point them in the right direction? The list of questions could go on and on.

How much time do you spend in front of new customers? Are you even set up to get in front of new customers? What's required to get in front of new customers? Where do your existing reps spend their time? Are they in front of existing customers or new prospective customers? I'm not talking about where you *think* they spend their time; I'm talking about where they actually spend their time.

Who did your Sales reps talk to yesterday? Who did they meet with last week? What were the results of the conversations and meetings they had last week? How many people did they talk with yesterday? How many appointments do they have this week? Do they have any open quotes?

If Sales is about finding new business from new customers, you better make sure your Sales reps are in front of new prospects.

As the Sales manager, you are responsible for managing Sales. And Sales now means "finding new business from new customers." What changes do you need to make? It's your job to make them. Where do you start?

I can imagine that you have a few thoughts, comments and questions racing through your mind. Hold on to them; we will address each of them.

Do you measure Sales by measuring new business from new customers? How much of your Sales rep's commission is based on new business from new customers? If you answer very little, then don't be surprised that you don't have much new business from new customers. If you answer that the majority of their commission is based on new business from new customers and you still don't have much new business, then you have a different problem.

Let me ask a very simple question; do you want new business from new customers? It seems silly to even ask the question. Of course you do. Every company I meet with is looking for new business from new customers. The ironic thing is that their Sales structure is so far the opposite of what they need and what they want. Why, then, do they not have a Sales structure that focuses on that? Why are they not set up to ensure that everything their Sales force does centers on finding new business from new customers? Instead, they sit back and simply hope it happens.

If your Sales Reps are not in front of new customers, then they are not selling according to our definition. If they are not selling, what are they doing? Hold your thought and your comment; we will address it.

Let's read my definition of Sales again and take it one step further.

"Sales focuses on finding and closing new business from new customers 100 percent of the time."

Step three says that Sales focuses on finding and closing new business from new customers. First we said that Sales means finding new business. Then we said Sales means finding new business from new customers. Now we've added that Sales means finding and *closing* new business from new customers.

Closing new business adds another whole dimension to our definition. Finding new business is one thing. Finding new business from new customers is another thing. Now you not only have to find it, but you also need to close it.

Well, guess what, it's Wednesday. You just showed up for work, and now your understanding of Sales is to *find* and *close* new business from new customers. Well, now you had better take a step back. Finding business and closing business are two different things. You need to think about how you're going to accomplish this.

Well, you can do like 99 percent of the companies out there do; hire Sales reps and tell them they need to go sell. You may give them certain existing accounts that you want them to manage, as well. Oh, one more thing. You may want to tell them to go to Walmart to get daily planners so they can track their activity. Tell them they can track it however they wish. Tell them that you don't really require them to track or report anything specific. Give them PCs and tell them to spend time on the Internet looking up companies to call because you really don't have any past data because you have never captured it. Wish them good luck and put them on their way.

Oh, one more thing. Tell them they can work out of their homes and that you have no means of monitoring if they are up and working by 8 a.m. and working until 5 p.m. And lastly, there is no requirement of how many calls they need to make or how many customers they need to see each week and month.

This sounds pretty blunt; however, this is what many and most companies do. My guess is that your company is not far from this, as well. I'm not being facetious. I see this every day of the week. It sounds pretty ridiculous, doesn't it?

Are your Sales reps closers? Are you confident that your Sales reps can close the deal? Are they aggressive enough to do this? Can they read the customer, hear what the customer is really telling them? Are they asking for the deal? Are they selling add-on products and services or leaving money on the table?

I have sat in meetings and heard companies openly admit that they don't want to send Sales rep A or Sales rep B on a lead because they don't have confidence they can close the deal. If that is the case then why are they working for you in a Sales capacity?

You're saying to yourself, my Sales reps do spend time prospecting for new business. It is part of their job. In fact, they may even have to send a weekly or monthly report to show who they have contacted. You're saying to yourself, we do a pretty good job of closing business.

Do you know how many meetings I have sat in and listened to a vice president of Sales try to convince me that he or she is on top of his or her Sales force? Do you know how many times I have heard that a company demands certain behaviors from its Sales reps and that it has complete knowledge of what its Sales force is doing?

If you are already set up for this, if your Sales reps are already prospecting for new business, then why are you reading this book? I can tell you why you are reading this book. Your Sales structure doesn't work. Your definition of Sales doesn't work, either. Your Sales reps are not accomplishing what you need them to do. You say they are prospecting for new business, but they really aren't, and you know it to be true. In fact, you are looking for an easy answer. Everyone is looking for an easy answer to Sales. I don't get it!

Hold your thoughts; we're getting to the heart of the matter. Let's finish the definition:

"Sales focuses on finding and closing new business from new customers 100 percent of the time."

Well, you're saying to yourself, I was OK when all I had to do was show up Monday morning and the definition of Sales was to *find new business*. You were OK with that, although it immediately caused you to rethink a few things.

But then when you showed up Tuesday, the definition changed. Now you had to *find new business from new customers*. OK you said, that refocuses me a little differently; but I'm still on track and I still have some ideas and thoughts.

Wednesday when you showed up for work you were charged with finding and *closing* new business from new customers. That throws a little curve. Finding the new business is a task all by itself. Closing it is another whole issue and concern.

And now lastly you're telling me that I have to do this *100 percent of the time*.

Well, it's Thursday morning, you just arrived to work, and the memo from the president says, "Attention Mr. VP Sales: moving forward, our Sales groups will focus on *finding and closing new business from new customers 100 percent of the time.*"

What are you going to do? Where do you start? What do you do about the other things that are important, as well, such as taking care of existing customers, account management, customer service, answering incoming calls, etc.?

The fact is, the reality is, the truth is, this is the definition of Sales. It has always been the definition of Sales. The definition of Sales has never changed. Why would you not want to find and close new business from new customers all the time?

Finding and closing new business from new customers is exactly what companies want from their Sales force. The irony of it all is that their Sales structure is not set up to accomplish the very thing they desire.

We lost sight of the true definition of Sales. We fell into the trap of being busy but not productive. We allowed our focus to get watered down. We allowed our Sales force to become unfocused and lazy. We allowed Sales to become all-inclusive.

When you define Sales this way, it becomes very easy to measure. Why would you want anything less from your Sales department?

I know what you're thinking. I told you to hold that thought; well, now we can address it.

You're thinking, "What about all the other aspects of Sales?" Well, according to our definition, the other things you are thinking of don't fall under Sales. If I use this definition of Sales, what do I do about my existing customers that require service and account management?

If taking care of existing customers is important, and we all know it is, how do I address that need? If answering incoming customer service calls is important, how do I handle that?

None of these focus on finding and closing new business from new customers 100 percent of the time. Therefore, don't include them in Sales.

The answer to how you handle these issues is quite simple.

It is the *Concept*!

CHAPTER 2

THE CONCEPT

**"Finding and closing new business from new customers needs
to be separated from all other Sales initiatives."**

It is important that we keep our new definition of Sales in front of us and fresh in our minds. If we are going to manage to this definition, then we need to determine what change or impact this will have on our Sales force. How does this definition of Sales change your current Sales structure? What does this mean for your existing customers?

If your Sales reps are spending their time and energy looking for new business from new customers, how will they have time to manage your existing customers? Your existing customers generate regular, ongoing revenue; you can't afford to put them on the back burner, you can't provide them lesser service than you have in the past, and you can't show them less attention than you have in the past. If you do, they will leave.

Before we begin to answer these questions, let's make sure we accept our new definition of Sales. Let's make sure that we truly understand what it is saying. If we truly understand our new definition of Sales, then we will truly understand the Concept.

From this point forward everything we talk about is based on the following definition of Sales:

**"Sales focuses on finding and closing new business
from new customers 100 percent of the time."**

This is the cornerstone for which we will base the remainder of this book. If you accept this definition, you have already taken the first step in improving your Sales structure.

Based on our definition of Sales, then yes, you may not have any Sales Reps in your organization. But you're thinking, who are all those people that work out of their homes? Who are those people that we pay commission to each month? Who are all those people that carry our business cards that have the titles account executive, account manager, regional Sales representative, and more?

Do they focus 100 percent of their time finding and closing new business from new customers? If the answer is no, then they are not Sales people. Remember, we are living to our new definition. As you can quickly see, this is going to cause you to rethink a few things.

The chances are the individuals you employ are account managers, customer service representatives, order entry clerks, and so on. Based on our definition of Sales, they do not fall under Sales. They fall under one of the other areas we just mentioned. However, who those people are is still a good question to ask. Perhaps you should have been asking that question long ago.

I contend that most companies truly don't employ Sales reps.

Remote Sales reps working out of their homes are the most inefficient, most costly, most mismanaged group within any organization. This isn't the fault of the remote Sales reps; it is the fault of the company who employs them.

I know this isn't always the case. I know there are instances where the Sales rep working from home happens to be a pretty good situation for both the employee and employer. However, as a rule, this is an area of inefficiencies that leaves great room for improvement.

I have the opportunity to meet with many companies of all sizes and industries. I meet with large supply-chain companies, software resellers, material handling companies, marketing and advertising, and more. Regardless of the size or type of company, the issue is the same. Their Sales force is not set up to accomplish the goals and objectives of the organization.

Why?

How does a company not have the right Sales structure? Sales is the heartbeat of any organization. If this is true, how is your Sales group anything less than 100 percent effective, efficient, productive, and designed to accomplish exactly what you need?

How is your Sales group not focused on the very thing you want them to do? The answer is simple. You have not defined Sales.

The responsibility is on you, the owner, the VP of Sales, or the person who is ultimately responsible for your Sales organization. You're the one that is supposed to know what you need and what you want. If you don't know what you need, what you want and a clear path of how you plan to get there, then don't expect your Sales reps to deliver what you need and what you want.

Contrary to some companies' beliefs, Sales doesn't just happen. Sales isn't an event; it is a process. Customers aren't knocking on your door waiting in line to buy your product or service. They're not spending their day trying to find you on the Internet so they can call you and place an order.

Don't fool yourself that you have the best product on the market. In some cases, having the best product or service doesn't matter. If it did, then why is there so much competition? Why doesn't everyone simply buy the best product or service?

If I had a nickel for every company that said to me, "We aren't the cheapest, but we have the best service," I could retire tomorrow.

If you are really serious about improving Sales, then there is one simple thing you need to understand. This simple thing is the Concept. The Concept states,

"Finding and closing new business from new customers needs to be a dedicated function."

Or in other words,

"Sales needs to be separated from all other initiatives."

Remember our definition of Sales: "Sales focuses on finding and closing new business from new customers 100 percent of the time."

The Concept is really quite simple, but typically not exercised. The Concept implies that Sales cannot be confused with or part of any other function in your organization. You cannot mix Sales and account management. You cannot combine Sales and customer service. You cannot blend Sales and order entry.

Quite simply, whoever you assign to Sales can have no other responsibility.

Sales focuses on finding and closing new business from new customers 100 percent of the time. The Concept states that this has to be separated from everything else. Sales is that important. It truly is the heartbeat of your organization.

The Concept has nothing to do with the fact that account management is extremely important. Improving customer relationships and increasing revenue inside existing accounts is essential to the success of any organization. It simply is not Sales; it is account management.

Taking care of and resolving customer issues is vital in keeping and maintaining long-term customer relationships. Customer service is imperative in maintaining brand loyalty. It simply is not Sales, it is customer service.

Effectively answering incoming calls from companies who want to buy your product or service is critical and necessary. Having knowledgeable personnel answering incoming calls and able to efficiently enter orders is necessary. It simply is not Sales; it is Order Entry.

When discussing Sales, most companies will group many positions and functions under the Sales umbrella. Below are some of the most common:

- Account Management
- Customer Service
- Order Entry
- Marketing
- Project Management
- Operations

I think it is safe to say that every one of the functions listed above can or does have a role in creating or servicing our customers. This is where the confusion, misconception, and problem begins.

Based on our definition, none of the functions listed above should be included in Sales. None of these areas focus on finding and closing new business, from new customers, 100 percent of the time.

Do I have your attention yet?

Account managers often are seasoned Sales reps. Typically, these individuals have been in the industry for many years. Generally, they are responsible for managing a territory, a vertical market, or specific named accounts. Most often, their job is to maintain relationships and to insure that their existing customers don't leave. The account managers are generally very experienced with their given industry.

The account manager often gets involved in customer service issues, contract negotiations, and general day-to-day needs to keep the account happy. This role becomes very important in large organizations. The account manager's customers often make up a large portion of the company's revenue. It is important to service these accounts and to maintain the relationships in an effort to keep them as customers.

Although the account manager's role is critical and necessary, it is important that we understand where and how it relates to the overall structure. It is not 100 percent focused on finding and closing new business from new customers. As a result, it should not be considered Sales.

One of the biggest mistakes companies make is tasking the account manager with prospecting for new business from new customers. The account manager says, "The last thing I want to do is pick up the phone and make a cold call." The account manager says, "I'm too busy. I don't have time to make cold calls."

Often the task of cold calling and prospecting for new business is below the account manager. At least it is in their eyes. Account managers often feel they have paid their dues, they are beyond cold calling, and they are not going to do it. They may generate new business within existing customers; they may find new business through a referral or through networking. But they aren't going to set time aside each day to make cold calls and prospect into new companies. Even if the company demands it, it isn't going to happen to the level it needs to; if it happens at all.

Why is this important to understand? The answer is simple. Companies operate with a false sense of security, believing that their account managers are prospecting for new business. They believe or want to believe they have a Sales force that is in the market each and every day seeking new business from new customers.

Even though the company tasks the account manager with new business development, it doesn't happen. The account manager spends his or her time with existing accounts. The account manager will find anything to do in an effort to keep busy before picking up the phone to make cold calls.

Even if you do get an account manager who is willing to make cold calls, he or she can't, won't, or doesn't make enough. He or she will not set aside enough time each day to have an impact.

Almost every company that I come in contact with has the same Sales structure. It has account managers that are tasked with managing existing accounts and prospecting for new accounts. This will never work to the degree we need it to. You are asking an account manager to be a hunter and a farmer. By nature, he cannot be both.

This is where the Concept comes into play. The Concept says,

**"Finding and closing new business from new customers
needs to be a dedicated function."**

Effective account managers are farmers by nature. They like nurturing accounts; they like the relationship side of Sales; they like the face-to-face interaction. They like the account management tasks and functions. These personality traits and characteristics are 180 degrees from the hunter.

The hunter is a hired gun. He likes the thrill of the hunt. He likes to prowl for the kill. He likes to seek new business. He likes to find the customer, make the sale, and move on. The hunter is bored with nurturing anything, and the thought of having to work with the same customer each and every day would drive him crazy.

The hunter likes hunting, capturing, and killing. Once he has accomplishes this, he is on to the next one.

Account managers can never be farmers and hunters at the same time. As a result, there is a weakness in the Sales force and Sales structure.

You may be thinking, "How do I support adding another layer to my Sales force? If my account managers aren't going to prospect for new business, then I need to hire someone or create a new group to do this. How do I support this additional cost?"

Most Sales organizations can add this structure and function with no additional cost. Yes, that is correct: with no additional cost. In fact, I contend that many Sales organizations could implement this at a lesser cost than their current structure.

How do we do that?

Most companies have account managers who are responsible for managing existing accounts, finding new accounts, customer service tasks, and more. Take the existing dollars you spend on this group and reallocate them. Instead of having ten account managers all responsible for account management, prospecting, customer service, and more, reduce that to five or what you feel is appropriate. Take the unused dollars and allocate that to new business development.

You may be saying to yourself, "How do I reduce my number of account managers without hurting the accounts in which they manage?"

The reality is that you have account managers in territories that are highly ineffective. You simply feel good that you physically have someone in the field rather than having the *right* person in the field.

I am confident you have inefficiencies within your Sales force that you can easily identify. Just as you are reallocating dollar resources, you must begin to reallocate job responsibilities and territory assignments.

You must identify your best account managers and determine how to better and more efficiently utilize them, their time and the territory or accounts they manage. This is something you should be doing anyway, regardless of anything you read in this book. If they are truly your best account managers, wouldn't you want them in front of as many of your existing customers as possible, especially your larger customers?

Under this Concept, you will have fewer account managers, but they will be more efficient. They will be busier than they were before because you have only kept the good ones, and they are now responsible for managing more customers. However, this is now 100 percent of their job responsibility. You will remove the task of new business development and prospecting for new business. They will spend 100 percent of their time managing and servicing existing accounts.

By removing the requirement of new business from them, you are freeing them up to spend more time with existing customers. As a result, they can manage more accounts. You need to take accounts from your underachievers and give them to your higher achievers. By eliminating your account managers that are underachievers, you free up dollars to add Sales reps who focus 100 percent of their time on finding and closing new business from new customers.

In theory, you can spend the same overall dollars and in fact have better overall coverage for existing customers as well as market penetration for new customers.

I understand that there is more to it than what I outlined in a few paragraphs. However, my goal at this point is not to lay out the complete structure, but rather the Concept. The structure is another book by itself.

You will need to evaluate how many Sales reps and account managers you need based on your company's needs and objectives. Remember, Sales reps now refer to people who are finding and closing new business from new customers 100 percent of the time.

It is probably safe to say that you do not have any Sales reps currently within your organization. The question becomes whether you outsource the Sales rep function or perform this function in-house. If your organization is not an aggressive, proactive Sales machine which uses CRM (Customer Relationship Management) software with great detail and conviction, then you need to outsource this function.

Managing a Sales group or new business development group is completely different from managing a group of account managers. If you're not sure whether you should outsource or do this in-house, I would suggest meeting with a few companies that provide this service. Find out from them, in detail, what they do and how they do it. Then you can make a determination of whether this is something you are comfortable with bringing in and managing in-house.

My company has been providing Sales services and Lead Management services since 2002. This is a very intense, complex, and administratively difficult process to manage. My experience is that most companies are not good at this process and therefore elect to outsource this vs. trying to manage it in-house.

When you implement an effective Sales or new business development team, you will quickly see your Sales pipeline begin to grow. Quote activity will begin to increase. You will become aware of opportunities that you would have not known about before. An effective new business development program will have a very positive effect on your overall Sales results.

Imagine for a moment that you have a team of Sales reps that are prospecting 100 percent of every day for new business from new customers. What effect would that level of daily effort and activity have on your overall Sales results? The answer is twofold. First of all, you don't know the answer because you have never done this before. You can't begin to quantify the answer because you simply don't know. The other answer is that this type of activity will have a very positive impact on your Sales. If hunting and prospecting for new business from new customers 100 percent of the time each and every day doesn't have a positive impact on your Sales activity, I am not sure what will.

It is not enough to understand and accept the Concept. Most companies I meet with agree with the Concept. Selling the idea of the Concept is not difficult. Getting companies to apply the Concept is where the rubber meets the road. Being willing to implement the Concept inside your organization is the test.

Are you willing to implement the Concept? Do you believe the Concept will change your overall Sales results? If you are serious about finding and closing new business from new customers, I think you need to seriously consider it.

Doing nothing is not an option. As the old saying goes, "If you continue to do what you have always done, you will continue to get what you always got." Just because you did things a certain way in the past is not a valid reason for you to continue doing it that way moving forward. Things change, times change, people change, the economy changes. The way we sell must change, too.

CHAPTER 3

YOU ARE ALLOWING UNDERACHIEVERS IN YOUR SALES FORCE

Many things in this chapter will probably hit home with you and your organization. We are going to address the real truth about Sales. We are going to admit to the things that everyone knows to be true but never addresses. We are going to get very specific; we are not going to hold anything back; and we are going to hit things head-on.

If you are an owner of a company, a CFO or CEO, you are going to look at things differently after reading this book. You may ask yourself, "Why haven't I looked at Sales this way before?" Some of you may agree 100 percent with the Concept; however, if I challenge you, my bet is that you don't manage to your belief.

If you are a VP of Sales or Sales manager, you'd better buckle up your bootstraps because this is your Sales organization we are talking about. Adopting the Concept will challenge you to approach Sales differently than ever before. The Concept will challenge you to do your job.

If you are a Sales rep, you will personally be able to relate to the Concept. You will understand exactly what I am presenting. You have experienced much of this firsthand. You have been there; you get it.

I have the opportunity to meet with many companies all across the country, companies from all industries and all sizes. The simple fact that I have an opportunity to meet with them already implies that they have a Sales need. Something in their organization is not going as planned.

With regard to the companies I meet with, the one thing they have in common is they all want more business. Every company would like to increase Sales. Most of all, they would like to increase Sales from new customers. The ironic thing is that their Sales structure is set up and structured for the complete opposite of what they want.

When I am asked to come and meet with a company, it is generally because they are seeking to generate new business and increase Sales. They have come to some conclusion that their existing Sales structure for whatever reason is unable to achieve the goals of the organization.

When companies reach this point, they have resolved that their current Sales structures are unable to achieve their goals, and as a result, they are looking for alternatives, suggestions, and options.

Today's market and economy have caused companies to rethink their Sales strategies. Companies no longer have the luxury of doing things like they did in the past. Times have changed, the market has changed, the competition has changed, and, yes, the consumer has changed, as well.

Specific industries, such as transportation, supply chain, and material handling, have drastically changed. Many companies in these industries grew and flourished through market demand. The market was good, the demand was high, and their products or services were in need.

Many of these companies responded to the needs in the market. Sure, they worked hard to provide a good service or a good product. However, the overall business climate was good. People were buying their products and services regularly. They did not have to turn over a lot of stones to find business.

Now, the market has done a 180-degree turn. The demand is no longer as great as it once was. These industries have to rethink how they are going to market their products and services. When the market was good and the demand was high, these companies could simply react and respond. Now, they are forced to be proactive. The market is no longer driving customers their way. These same companies are now being forced to aggressively find new customers and new ways of generating business.

Companies are seeing their customer base shrink. Their customer base that once generated $500 million in revenue may now only generate $250 million. Not only has it shrunk, but it doesn't have the ability of returning to $500 million. Companies are forced to find new ways of generating Sales. They come to a conclusion that in order to return to $500 million in Sales, they need to find new business from new customers. As they assess their existing Sales staff, they realize they don't have the right type of Sales reps. Their Sales force consists primarily of account managers that were good at managing that $500 million customer base. They find themselves with account managers that were good when the business came to them. They were good at managing it and servicing it. However, the market has changed. These same account managers are required to go out and prospect for new business, and specifically from new customers.

The company says, "I don't need as many account managers as I did six to twelve months ago. I don't need as many farmers as I used to. What I need is hired guns; I need hunters. The only way I am going to get back to $500 million is to find new business from new customers, and to do that I need hunters." This is causing companies to restructure their Sales force.

When I meet with new clients, I spend a lot of time trying to understand their Sales goals and objectives. I have them share with me what they are trying to accomplish and why. I inquire about their existing Sales structure. They have a Sales force; they employ account managers. What is not working? Why did they feel compelled to bring in an outside resource to help them accomplish an objective or to reach a goal?

During every meeting, I get to the point where I ask the same three questions. This inquiry quickly gets to the truth. I have yet to experience a Sales call where these three questions haven't cut to the heart of the matter.

In a matter of a minute, I am quickly able to get a pulse of their Sales force and the manager(s) in charge. This process helps me determine the mentality of the company that is considering utilizing my service. It helps me assess if their problem is their structure, management, or both.

When I meet with a prospective client, I ask the following:

Question 1: *"How many Sales reps to you have?"*

Knowing the size of the Sales force helps me get a sense of the scale of the problem and the challenge of addressing the problem. It also helps me identify how big of a group the manager is managing. Regardless of how the prospect responds, it doesn't change my next question. It doesn't matter if they say they have five, ten or a hundred Sales reps. My following question is always the same.

Question 2: *"What percentage of your Sales force would you consider to be lower than average performers?"*

The answer to this question never varies. It is the same 100 percent of the time. It is this response that causes me to shake my head in disbelief every time I hear it. Their response is the primary reason I formed Concept Services. I look forward to getting to this point on all new Sales calls.

Their response is 30 percent to 50 percent! In fact, I have had prospects say they believe as much as 50 percent or 75 percent of their Sales force is made up of lower-than-average performers. Not only is the response the same each time I ask the question, but the delivery of the response is identical, as well. The prospect never hesitates to answer. In cases where I have had several employees from the prospect in the room, each will respond the same and at the same time. It is almost like they have known the answer for the past year or two.

What really troubles me are the positions and titles of the individuals who are responding. I typically meet with owners, VPs of Sales, CEOs, and CFOs. So, the top executives in the company are responding and admitting that a large portion of their Sales force is made up of lower-than-average performers.

I wonder if they would continue operating a machine in their factory if that machine kept producing scrap parts. I wonder if they would continue running a truck in their fleet if it was unsafe or always breaking down and caused late pickups and deliveries.

This leads me to my third question.

Question 3: *"If you believe that 30 percent to 50 percent of your Sales force is comprised of underachievers and lower-than-average performers, then why do you keep them?"*

After I ask this question, the room becomes silent. No one really knows how to respond. In unison, they all agreed that a large percent of their Sales staff are underachievers. The fact that they all answered in unison means there is obviously no doubt or question regarding the validity of their answer.

The individuals that are responding this way are the owners, the VPs of Sales, and the CFOs. They are the individuals that should know what is going on. It is their opinion that really matters. These are the people that have the ability to make decisions; they can make changes, but they aren't. Why? I guess accepting less than average is acceptable in their company.

Well, this is where the truth comes in. The reason they have 30 percent, 40 percent, or 50 percent of their Sales staff listed as underachievers and underperformers is because the president, VP of Sales, CFO, and owner are not doing their job. If they were doing their job, this would have never happened, and they would not be allowing one-third or one-half of their Sales staff to be underachievers.

I can guarantee you they wouldn't allow someone in accounting that was less than average continue to manage their books. I am sure if the books weren't balancing month after month, they would make a change in accounting.

I am sure they wouldn't allow a machine operator who continually produces a high percent of scrap each month to continue running the machine. They would find a new operator.

I am sure if one of their machines required maintenance every month, they would find a way to replace it or get it fixed once and for all.

I am sure if one of their delivery drivers were late on deliveries month after month, they would make a change with the driver.

I am sure if the computer network continued to cause problems every month, they would find a way to get it fixed or replace the person responsible for maintaining the network.

But when it comes to Sales, they somehow tolerate below average. They allow that which would be unacceptable in any other part of the business to be accepted in Sales.

Why?

Maybe it's because they don't know what to do. Maybe they think it will fix itself or improve on its own. Maybe it's because they are lazy and are not doing their jobs as Sales managers, presidents, or owners. Whatever the reason, the fact is that they have underachievers in their Sales force. Doing nothing doesn't fix the problem.

Truth #1—You are allowing underachievers to exist in your Sales force.

CHAPTER 4

YOU ARE AFRAID TO MAKE
THE NECESSARY CHANGES

If you have ever worked in a production or manufacturing environment, then you know there are immediate consequences for operating a machine incorrectly or falling behind on an assembly line. When a machine is operated incorrectly, several things can happen: the machine can break; the machine can't produce as many parts as it should; you can produce defective parts; you can fall short in fulfilling orders; you can increase the chances of injury; and the list goes on.

As soon as that machine goes down, as soon as that production line stops, as soon as that machine begins producing defective parts, management stops what they are doing to address the issue. They respond immediately. They see lost dollars. They see deadlines being missed, shipments being missed, upset customers, employees standing around getting paid to do nothing, and more.

Companies have tools in place to manage the output of their machines and production as a whole. They know what is produced each and every day. They are monitoring trends as they compare week to week and month to month. They know when they need to address an issue. They even have regular maintenance schedules to keep the machines in proper working condition.

Why don't we manage Sales to this level?

There are immediate consequences when the accountant isn't doing his or her job correctly. Imagine, for a moment, an accounts payable clerk for a Fortune 1000 company deciding to slack off. As a result, she does not stay on top of her tasks. I'm not implying that she is home sick or on vacation. I'm implying that she still comes to work for those days, but since no one is really monitoring what she does, she decides to slack off and not perform the tasks and functions of her job.

What would happen? The company would begin receiving calls from angry vendors inquiring when they will be paid. Next, vendors will refuse to continue providing services until they are paid. Production and other aspects of the company will then be affected. If this type of behavior went on for a month or two, there would be significant consequences.

If accounting doesn't do their job on a daily basis, the books don't balance at the end of the month. Employees don't get paid on time. Checks begin to bounce. Employees and vendors begin to question the status of the company.

Management manages this area to a tee. They know what is going on at all times. They understand that they can't afford to let this area go without attention. There are daily tasks that must get executed each and every day.

Management has reports that tell them exactly where every dollar was spent. They know exactly how much was spent on every aspect of the business. They know how much they have paid to each and every Sales rep. They know how much commission was paid and how much expenses were paid. They know how much was spent on raw materials, inventory, etc. They have a pulse on every financial aspect of their business.

Why don't we manage Sales to this level?

We are in an era where having Sales reps working out of their homes is the norm. This structure started years ago as companies tried to reduce costs. The idea was that the company didn't need to provide an office or cube for their Sales rep. It seemed to make sense to have people work out of their homes in the geographic regions where the company wanted to sell their product or service. If they lived in the region, it would cut down on travel costs. They could spend more time out in front of their customers.

What a problem this has caused. How do you know if your remote Sales reps who work out of their homes are even out of bed and working by 8 a.m.? I know of cases where Sales reps get up, send a few emails to the corporate office and customers between 7 and 7:30 a.m. simply to appear as if they are up and at it. Then, they go back to bed or they go take care of personal business. However, the corporate office or Sales manager sees activity early in the morning and assumes the Sales rep is working.

How often are your remote Sales reps quitting early to cut the grass or to work on a household project? Since everyone is remote and has a smart phone, the remote Sales rep can make it appear as if he or she is working anytime. In fact, he or she may be sitting by the pool.

How do you know what they are really doing? How productive are they during the day? One of the arguments is that field Sales reps work late in the evenings and on the weekends. This may be true; however, I would suggest that if they were doing what they needed to do during the hours of 8 a.m. and 5 p.m., most of them would not have to work late into the evenings or on the weekends.

When it comes to Sales, we don't have the same level of control or information that we have in other areas of the organization. We have Sales reps that go days, maybe weeks, without us really knowing what they are doing. Why? What are your Sales reps doing? The fact of the matter is that, in most cases, we don't know.

Why don't you manage your Sales force to the same level as your accounting department?

Why don't you manage your Sales force to the same level as your production department?

Why don't you manage your Sales force to the same level as your HR department?

Most companies rely on their Sales reps to tell them what they are doing. I have yet to have a Sales person tell me that he isn't working. I have never had a Sales rep tell me the reason she is not hitting quota is because she isn't working very hard. I've never had a Sales rep tell me that his Sales are down because he doesn't get started every morning until 10 a.m. and quits at 3:30 p.m. I've never had a Sales rep admit that she is content with her salary and really doesn't care if she sells anything because the income she receives based on her salary is sufficient for her.

Typically we hear things like "The market is tough," "No one has any budget," "Everyone is telling me to call back in six months," and the list goes on. I've been in Sales a long time; trust me when I say I am not exaggerating.

I want to see the accounts they called on that are telling them this. It may very well be true, but I want to see it. Have ten of the last twelve companies told them that, or have they heard it once in the past few weeks? I want to see data. I want to see proof.

Can you imagine the controller going into a board meeting and saying, "We spent $100,000 last month on expenses"? In response, one of the board members asks, "Where was it spent?" The controller responds, "I don't know for sure, but I think it was $50,000 on advertising, $15,000 on general admin, $10,000 on fuel, $20,000 on maintenance and repair, and $5,000 on phone expense." The board member then says, "Let me see the report that breaks this down." The controller replies, "I don't have a report, but I know this is pretty accurate." That would fly like a lead balloon. But that's what we do in Sales. If you're going to take the Sales rep's word for it, why not take the controller's word for it? What's the difference?

You may say that there are serious and fairly quick consequences for allowing accounting to go unmanaged. Let me inform you, the consequences for allowing Sales to go unmanaged are just as serious.

Without Sales, we don't need accounting!

How do we know what the Sales rep is saying is accurate? Is it one company that has said to call back in six months? Is it nine of the last ten companies that have said that to them? How many companies have they contacted in the past sixty days?

When accounting says, "We spent $100,000 on expenses last month," you don't simply say "OK"; you want to see a breakdown of where you spent those dollars. You then know for a fact that the number is accurate and valid. As a result, you can make informative and educated decisions.

Why do we allow our Sales reps to go unmanaged? There was a day when Sales Reps were prima donnas. They were off-limits. Whatever they said was gospel. Nobody really knew what they did during the day, and they were seldom challenged.

I never quite understood that. It didn't make sense then, and it definitely doesn't make sense today. Sales reps need to be managed to the same level of detail as the accounting department, the operations group, and any other position within the organization.

You would not allow your accounting group to go unmanaged for a month at a time, but that is exactly what many companies do with their Sales reps. I would suggest that in many cases, the Sales reps go unmanaged all the time, not just a month at a time.

Most companies wouldn't permit our accounting department to do everything on paper and ledger sheets. But that's what they allow their Sales force to do. Why?

When a production line goes down, there are immediate consequences. The line gets attention immediately. When the accountant doesn't do his job right, the books don't balance, and there is an immediate consequence. It gets addressed immediately.

However, when a Sales rep isn't performing, there is no immediate consequence. The consequences are down the road. In fact, in most cases, we don't even recognize they are not performing until Sales begin to slow down. The Sales pipeline slowly begins to dry up. Then, all of a sudden, the Sales forecast begins to look bad.

In most cases, by the time companies begin to realize they have a Sales problem, it is too late. The pipeline is dry, the forecast is bad, and cash flow is not good.

Isn't it funny? When Sales are down and cash flow is tight, everyone looks at Sales. From the top down, everyone wants to focus on Sales and begins to look at what the Sales reps are doing or not doing. New ideas are generated, and new plans are executed that will hopefully turn things around. However, when things are going well, no one even looks at what the Sales reps are doing. Everyone simply assumes things are going well.

Are things going well because you sold one large account? Are things going well because people are finding you on the Internet? Are things going well because you are getting new business from referrals? Are things going well because you announced a new product and there is a big demand for it? Are things going well because you simply have a dynamite Sales force, and they are bringing in new business from new customers?

Are things going well because your existing customer base is buying more products or services?

Do you even know why things are going well?

Did you ever sit back and evaluate, during these times, what real contribution your Sales reps are adding? Don't misunderstand me; we all need Sales reps. But we only need the ones that are selling and putting forth the effort each and every day. You should easily be able to tell if your Sales reps are having an impact on your Sales.

Most Sales organizations have no process in place to monitor Sales activity on a daily, weekly, or monthly basis. It's usually a matter of waiting till the end of the year and then wondering what happened. Often, we wait until it is too late and then say, "What are we going to do next year so this doesn't happen again?" And lastly, we often blame it on the economy or other external factors.

Perhaps we didn't hit our Sales goals because we didn't manage to them on a daily, weekly, or monthly basis. Maybe we didn't hit our Sales goals because we didn't do anything differently from how we've been doing it for the past umpteen years. Maybe we didn't hit our Sales goals because we didn't have any Sales goals.

Maybe, just maybe, we didn't hit our Sales goals because we don't have an effective Sales engine inside our organization. Maybe we didn't hit our Sales goals because we don't have an effective Sales manager or president who is driving the company.

How many times have you been asked to provide Sales goals for the upcoming year? What do you do? Well, you look at last year and then come up with a number that will be accepted for this year. You really don't have a good plan for how you are going to achieve it, other than "We are going to really work harder this year." Oh, I forgot, you may have even changed the Sales reps' compensation plans, thinking that will make them work harder.

Then, you have an annual Sales kickoff meeting in which you spend a lot of money to bring all of your Sales reps in from across the country. Remember at least one-third of these individuals are underachievers. However, you continue to spend money to fly them around the country and put them up in a hotel.

You have your big Sales meeting, spend a lot of dollars, and let everyone know what the goals are for next year. Each Sales rep gets his or her new quota, and that is it. Nothing really changes. They all go back to working out of their homes, doing the same thing they did for the past several years that didn't meet those goals, either.

The new year gets kicked off; all of the Sales reps have a fun time at the meeting and dinner. They all order drinks all night at the company's expense. Once they get their new quotas, they all have their own private conversations talking about how ridiculous the new quotas are and that the company doesn't understand and that the quotas are unattainable. They complain about the new comp plan and how it is unfair. You end your meeting, and everyone goes home. It's business as usual.

Did I miss anything?

How are you supposed to increase Sales when you're not changing anything? How are you supposed to increase Sales with the same staff you have had for the past several years when you didn't hit your Sales goals? You're not doing anything differently. How does the old saying go? "If you continue to do what you have always done, you will continue to get what you've always got."

Truth #2—Sales is the most mismanaged group in your organization.

CHAPTER 5

YOU ARE NOT SERIOUS ABOUT SALES

Are you serious about Sales? Are you really committed to making your Sales force better? If I asked this question to ten companies, probably a minimum of eight out of ten would say "yes." So why is it that nine out of ten companies I meet have no customer relationship management (CRM) solution to manage their Sales force? Then, to make it worse, the one company out of ten that does have a CRM solution doesn't use it.

When I walk into a company and they have no CRM solution, it speaks volumes about their Sales manager, president, and entire Sales organization. They are not serious about Sales. They say they are, but they're not investing in it.

How does the old saying go? "Your actions are so loud, I can't hear what you say." There isn't one company I meet with that doesn't have an accounting system to manage the financial side of their organization. All of them have software to manage their production, their inventory, and every other aspect of the organization. But once again, when it comes to Sales, they have no means to measure or monitor the daily, weekly, and monthly activity of their Sales reps. Why?

I'm not talking about measuring how much someone sold. That is easy. I'm talking about measuring their activity on a day-to-day basis. Sales is the heartbeat of our organizations, and yet we don't manage it that way. In fact, in some cases, I'm not sure we really manage it at all.

Why does a CFO demand that he or she have an accounting system to manage day-to-day activity? On second thought, the CFO doesn't have to demand it; the company simply provides it because it is necessary. It is necessary because there are a lot of things a CFO has to manage that would take extremely long if done manually. Also, the CFO wants a tool to help him more efficiently, effectively, and accurately manage.

The Sales manager who has a group of Sales reps and doesn't have a CRM tool isn't managing to the level he or she needs to. The department is inefficient, the same way accounting would be inefficient if they did not have a system to manage the financial side of the business.

You may be thinking that accounting has to have software to manage because they need to track costs, revenue, etc. They must track revenue coming in and expenses going out.

I'm here to tell you that Sales is no different. Sales, too, should be tracking effort going in and results coming out. This is as much a daily transaction as anything that accounting does.

Sales isn't an event; it is a process. The process must be managed the same as the accounting process must be managed.

If you are a Sales manager and you aren't monitoring what your Sales reps are doing on a daily basis, what are you managing? If you don't know what your Sales reps are doing every day, what are you doing? If you don't know who they called today and who they are scheduled to call later this week and month, what are you managing? Are you waiting until you get to the end of the quarter, realize that you are not hitting your numbers, and then try to figure out why?

Accounting exists because someone at some point sold something. As a result, there needed to be a means of managing what they sold, how many they sold, to whom they sold it, and what price they sold it for. There also needed to be a method and process to invoice it and to record payment.

Without Sales, we don't need accounting. Why is it that accounting gets so much attention, but the front end of that whole process, Sales, doesn't get the same level of attention? Without Sales, accounting doesn't even exist. Am I the only one that looks at it this way?

When your company first started, the most important thing was to find a customer. Why? If you couldn't get a customer, you didn't have a business. Everything focused on getting a customer. What has changed? I understand that you now have customers and you must take care of them, but that should not replace finding new customers.

If you were serious about managing Sales, if you were serious about driving performance, you would have a CRM solution. But don't think that simply because you have a CRM tool, your Sales will improve. Quite the contrary; most companies that I meet who do have a CRM tool don't even use it, and the implementation of it is a disaster.

So, either they don't have a CRM tool or they do have one and don't use it. That's like telling your accounting staff they can enter their transactions in Microsoft Outlook if they want to or in their daily planner. Or how about this: don't require your accounting group to enter any information anywhere. That's what we do with our Sales reps.

Think about how ludicrous that sounds. Can you imagine telling your accounting staff they can enter information into their daily planner? Perhaps I am being a little facetious, but the principle remains.

Why don't companies that have CRMs use them? I have witnessed many companies that have spent lots of money to implement a CRM solution to simply let it sit on their PCs unused. Why?

One of the reasons is because the older Sales reps don't want to use it. They complain that it takes too long to enter information. Their attitude is that they have never used CRM in the past, and they are not going to learn now. They are not computer-literate, so they struggle and find it time-consuming. They don't want the corporate office monitoring what they do on a daily basis. They feel they own their accounts and don't want to disclose all the information.

You know what I say about that? "Go find another job."

It isn't up to the Sales reps to determine what they are and are not going to do. Did they forget that the company sets the direction and the requirements? Did they forget that they work for the company, and the company doesn't work for them? The last time they looked at their paychecks, did they notice who signed it?

Things change, our needs change, and people need to change, too. Many companies struggle because their Sales force is just downright ineffective. They have no structure, no direction, and, as a result, no Sales. It is time for things to change from the top down.

Most often, reps don't want to use a CRM because they are not PC-literate or they don't want to be accountable. We can address the PC-literate part. We can help people get up to speed. We can train people how to do things.

If reps don't want to be accountable, then they are in the wrong position and need to find a new job.

During a meeting with one of our clients, the director of corporate accounts explained to us how he was a strong believer in CRM and truly understood the value of it. When we asked him to provide us an update on the 150 leads we submitted to his Sales reps over the past eighteen months, he was unable. He did not know. None of his Sales reps updated the CRM with any notes on the status of the leads. In fact, his own staff didn't even use CRM.

This client was adamant that everything we did had to get documented in their CRM. They would not work with us unless we agreed to log in and work within their CRM solution each day. So for almost two years, we religiously logged all our calls, emails, and other activity in their CRM. We documented everything to the nth degree and operated according to their requests and guidelines.

I expressed to the director of corporate accounts that if any Sales rep did not update the CRM, then the lead should be taken away from that rep. He quickly told me to be careful because I was referring to one of his number-one Sales reps. Once again, the Sales rep was a prima donna.

Doesn't make sense.

But wait a minute; let's not make the Sales reps out to be the culprit. Let's not lay the blame on them for not using the CRM. Sure, they buck the system. Yes, they bellyache and complain. But let's make sure we bring it into perspective.

The number-one reason companies don't use a CRM tool is because the Sales manager does not demand that it be used. The Sales manager should be the one driving this initiative. He or she is the reason a CRM is not implemented and used.

Many times, I find that the Sales manager is not familiar with technology, so he or she allows the Sales force to be inefficient. I'm not talking about using a Blackberry. Sometimes, I think the Blackberry is the best and worst thing that ever happened. (How many times have you sat in a meeting, and the person across the table is playing on his Blackberry? You know that he is not listening to a thing you are saying. He is more interested in sending emails back and forth than in giving you his attention.)

You don't have to be a technical genius to drive technology in your group. There are lots of companies out there that are more than capable of helping you. You don't have to be the one who knows how to physically set up a CRM. You don't have to be the one who knows how to implement it. However, as the head of Sales, you need to be the one who knows how to use it and understands the value and benefit of it.

A Sales force is an image of the manager. People will follow when led. When no one is leading, the troops will wander. As the Sales manager, your job is to lead. Your job is to set the example. Most of all, your job is to generate Sales for your company. Being a leader isn't easy. Getting the most out of your Sales force is your mission.

You may be reading this and saying, "We don't have the money to implement a CRM solution. The budget is tight. We are cutting back." I respond to that by saying that you can't afford not to.

I implemented a complete CRM solution for twenty-plus users inside my own company for about $400 per user. I can assure you, you are spending more than $400 per user per year in mismanaging your Sales force, with lost production and lost data.

There are many CRM solutions on the market. When boiled down, all of them do about 90 percent of the same thing. Don't get caught up in all of the bells and whistles that drive the price up. Don't get caught up in having to have the best solution on the market. There are many solutions to choose from.

If you are going to implement a CRM solution, meet with a company that uses CRM religiously. Don't just meet with a reseller. The problem with resellers is just that—they are resellers. They are not often the best users. Also, if you implement a CRM solution, don't stop everything else until it is implemented.

My partner and I met with a large, national company to discuss our lead generation services. It was our first meeting. After presenting our services, the person we met with turned around and showed us a proposal that he had on his credenza from a company just like ours.

He proceeded to tell us that our timing was perfect. He had been searching for an effective new business development company. He was looking for a company that could generate qualified leads for his Sales force.

He shared that he had been working on this initiative for several months. He had even traveled across the country to meet with companies like ours to see what they had to offer. After the meeting, he invited us to come back to meet with him and the CFO. This was a very large, very well known national company.

About six weeks later, my partner and I returned to give a full-blown presentation to another group of people. After the meeting, our contact shared that they really needed to move forward with the initiative. He went on to say that they wanted to implement a CRM solution as well and wanted to wait until the CRM solution was up and running before moving forward with generating leads.

Why would you ever put generating leads on hold?

A year and a half later, they were still playing around with their CRM solution. The solution was not fully up and running, their Sales reps were not using it, and guess what? They still needed leads.

Your number-one goal is to generate Sales. Don't ever put generating leads on the back burner.

Implementing a CRM solution by itself does not increase Sales. Creating a new business development or lead generation program by itself does not generate Sales. Effectively managing a Sales force, aggressively penetrating the market, demanding performance from your Sales staff, having specific goals and the right people in the right positions are what impact your Sales.

If you do not have a CRM tool in your organization, I don't know how you know what is going on within your Sales group.

Truth #3—You have no Sales tools because you are not serious about Sales and you don't understand the value and benefits a CRM solution can offer.

CHAPTER 6

GOALS AND KPIS

Without the proper tools in place, it is really tough to measure goals. Sure, we can tell if we hit our yearly numbers. That is pretty easy; we either did or we didn't. However, when you are in month three of a twelve-month goal, how do you really know where you are other than the bottom number? How do you know if you're doing all the right things? How do you know if your Sales reps are doing the daily things necessary in order to meet the quarterly and annual goals?

You need goals. You need measurable, attainable goals. You need metrics that you monitor on a daily, weekly, and monthly basis. I am referring to goals that are stepping stones to reach the main objective. I'm not referring to pie-in-the-sky goals. I am referring to daily and monthly activities designed to meet your ultimate goal and objective.

In our company we call them key performance indicators, or KPIs. The KPIs let me know if I am doing the right things along the way. They let me know if my Sales force is doing what they need to do on a daily basis in order to meet my monthly, quarterly and annual goals. My KPIs allow me to foresee a potential problem before it becomes a problem and to make adjustments to get back on track.

My KPIs enable me to see each day if my Sales force is doing what they need to do to meet the end goal. In order to reach my goals, I know that each of my Sales reps (we call them business development managers, or BDMs) need to generate X number of appointments. In order to generate X number of appointments, I need to have X number of qualified conversations on the phone. In order to have X number of qualified conversations, I need to make X number of calls per day.

In order to make X number of calls per day, I know I need to make X number of calls per hour.

The benefit of the KPIs is that they won't allow you to get too far down the road before realizing you need to make some changes. They also provide a means of measuring everyone against the same barometer or standard.

In my organization, I publish our KPIs weekly. All of my BDMs know each week where they are relative to their peers and their own personal goals.

It took over a year before the KPI report really began to mean something to the BDMs. It took time to drive home what we were trying to accomplish. We had a lot of pushback along the way. And yes, some BDMs were not willing to work toward the KPIs, and yes, we had to let them go and find BDMs that were willing to work within our standards.

It took time to really determine the right KPIs. I know what I wanted my end goal to be, but it took time to determine how to get there. Even though there was trial and error along the way, during the process we were still better than we were with no KPIs. Even though we had hurdles to jump over, each month we continued to get closer to where we needed to be.

The simple fact of having everyone marching to the same drum made us better. The KPIs made everyone focus on the same goal. Everyone was being measured the same. It provided a sense of direction and unity in the group. The KPIs are designed to meet certain goals and objectives, and having everyone in the organization working toward the same goals made us immediately stronger as an organization.

Now, the KPI report is our Sales Bible. Performance is based on the KPIs, commission is based on the KPIs, and weekly incentives are based on the KPIs. Our group has learned that the KPI report is gospel.

Don't be mistaken; having KPIs is only effective if you are going to manage to them. This is where having a CRM becomes a vital tool. Our CRM provides real-time dashboards for every KPI we monitor and measure.

If you're not familiar with the term "dashboard," let me explain. Think of your dashboard in your car. You have a dash that shows you how much gas you have. You have a dash that shows the temperature of your engine. Your dashboard shows your speed, miles per gallon, miles till empty, miles traveled, etc.

The Sales dashboard is the same concept. You set up what types of things you want to view. We view total calls made by BDMs. Not only do we monitor how many calls, but we monitor the status of the calls. In other words, was there a conversation or simply a voicemail? Remember that earlier, I said I know that I need to have X number of conversations in order to get an appointment. Therefore, I monitor not only how many calls my BDMs are making, but also how many conversations they are having with decision-makers. We have several different KPIs that we monitor each and every day.

You can set up your dashes to monitor just about anything. If you have outside reps, you may want to monitor who they have met with this week. You may want to monitor who they have reached out to this week. You may want to monitor how many companies they have met with in the past week or month. Are they meeting with enough companies in order to hit their goals? Also, what is the result of these meetings?

You can set up a dash to track proposals, as well as the Sales stages and Sales funnel. You can monitor customer service issues. Perhaps your organization is one that receives a lot of incoming calls from customers placing orders, and you want to track the number of incoming calls and orders placed for the day or for the hour, etc.

A dashboard is a visual tool that allows you to see, at a glance, the pulse of your Sales organization.

Most companies set Sales goals. Often, companies will share with me that their goal this year is X dollars. Or their goal is to exceed last year's goal by X percent. However, when you talk to them about how they are going to achieve it or what they have put in place that insures success, they haven't done anything. Their Sales activities this year are the same as last year. Their process is the same as it has always been. The Sales reps who did not meet quota last year are the same reps they have this year.

It sounds good to have a goal. How often are goals set, and then forgotten after a month or two? At least, it isn't at the forefront of every Sales person's thoughts. Everyone quickly falls right back into the same old routine of the past several years.

Having long-term Sales goals isn't enough. You need to have intermediate goals along the way. You need to have goals that reps can shoot for and achieve. You need to have KPIs that help measure their journey and don't allow you to get too far off course before needing to make adjustments.

Sales reps need to be managed closely, encouraged regularly, inspired often, and led by example.

Truth #4—You don't have goals, or the right goals, and you don't have KPIs to keep you on track.

CHAPTER 7

DO YOU HAVE THE RIGHT SALES MANAGER?

Let's briefly discuss leadership. Leadership is critical for any Sales organization. Sales reps need to believe in the organization and their Sales manager. The Sales manager, in turn, must know how to lead.

A common mistake is promoting someone to Sales manager simply because they have done well as a Sales rep. A good Sales person doesn't necessarily make a good manager. A good basketball player won't necessarily be a good coach.

Often, Sales reps are successful because they like working alone. They like doing their own thing. They like the fact that they are not working at a desk. They don't like planning, strategizing, and budgeting. Often, they don't like confrontation and don't handle it well. They don't like going into business meetings and talking about problems and plans. They want to be in front of the customer. They want to close a sale. They like working alone.

The qualifications of a Sales manager are much different from the qualifications of a Sales rep. Some of the most successful coaches in professional sports never played professional sports. However, they understand the game, they see a bigger picture, they know how to manage and motivate people, and they know how to get the job done.

Good Sales managers need to drive their Sales force. They need to know how to get the most out of people. They need to know at all times what is going on within their Sales force. They should be evaluating direction, results, efforts, and personnel at all times.

Owners and presidents should be comfortable that they have the right person in place to lead their Sales force. The Sales manager's job is to make sure the goals of the organization are being met.

Is your Sales manager a leader? Is he/she proactively leading the Sales organization? Is he/she leading by example? Is he/she allowing underachievers to be employed? Is he/she set up with the right tools? Is he/she a good mentor? Is he/she meeting her Sales goals? If he/she doesn't have tools in place, then he/she is not serious about managing Sales. Maybe he/she is serious about it but simply doesn't know how to get it done.

I often find Sales managers to be lazy. Obviously, I have seen many that are quite effective. However, if I made a blanket statement, I would say that most companies have the wrong Sales manager in place.

This comment isn't made lightly. I have worked with hundreds of companies in the past ten years. I have worked with companies of all sizes and industries. I'm telling you that most companies have the wrong Sales manager in place. Why do I say that?

Sales Managers need to lead by example. They need to set the vision and then move toward meeting the goals. They need to have an effective Sales approach, process, and team. I can assure you that many of the companies that I have been involved with do not have an effective Sales approach. They do not have an efficient process. They don't manage according to daily KPIs or metrics. They allow ineffective Sales reps to stay around too long. They have not put the necessary tools in place to effectively manage a Sales group.

We have a tagline on our organization that says, "It's not about closing the Sales today; it's about building the pipeline for tomorrow." Think about this before you respond to it.

I often find Sales organizations are living for today: "What can we do today to get Sales?" They are not forward-thinkers. They are very reactive instead of proactive. They are always looking for low-hanging fruit. There is not a Salesperson or Sales manager out there that doesn't like it when he finds low-hanging fruit. Don't get me wrong; I, too, love when I come across something that was easy to get.

A successful Sales manager, however, needs to have a plan that provides for regular, ongoing business. He needs to do whatever he can to prevent the valleys in the Sales cycle. In a perfect world, Sales would always be level and consistent. We would never experience the highs and lows. However, that is not the real world of Sales.

That being said, I believe there are lots of things a successful Sales Manager can do to prevent the lows from being too low. A company should never underestimate the value of an effective Sales manager. The right person in the right place can have a tremendous impact on Sales.

A Sales manager needs to ensure she is getting the most out of her Sales force. We already established that organizations are employing below-average Sales Reps. If you are an effective Sales manager, why are you allowing this to happen?

Sales reps are like children. They watch what happens around them. They learn what they can and cannot get away with, and then they find ways to beat the system.

When you allow poor performance by just one Salesperson, you bring down the entire group. You lower the bar for everyone.

You can be confident that everyone within your Sales organization can easily identify the strong performers and the weak performers. They know who is lying and cheating and who is trying to beat the system. They know who works hard and who is trying to be the best they can be.

When you don't address the problem areas, your staff begins to question you. When you allow things to go on that shouldn't, they begin to question what is really important and what isn't. They begin to wonder if you know what is going on. If so, then they wonder why you are not addressing it. You quickly begin to lose integrity. It is at this point that employees begin to lose respect for their Sales manager and the overall integrity of the organization.

I believe people want to work for an organization that stands for something. I believe people want to work for someone who is dedicated to doing his or her best. I believe that employees want to work for a company that has integrity and demands performance. When people perform well, they feel good about themselves.

The integrity of an organization is torn down by employing underachievers and allowing bad behavior.

I can speak firsthand to this issue. I have learned by mistakes. I have allowed things to happen longer than I should. I have seen smoke turn to fire, and I have been burned. I have done this more than once and have learned my lesson.

In my organization, we generate leads and Sales opportunities for our clients. Our BDMs are on the phone all day hunting for new business opportunities for our clients. It is critical that they make their calls and talk to as many people as they can in an effort to find an opportunity that matches our client's need. That's what we get paid to do.

I want to share a story of a BDM who, for the sake of this story, we will call Steve. The story is real; the names have been changed.

Steve was always very loud on the phone. He was actually pretty good. When we hired Steve, he hit the ground running. He worked hard and quickly stood out among his peers.

Steve was hitting his goals and seemed to be doing everything right. He would arrive to work every morning at 7:45 a.m.; we started at 8 a.m. He was always positive and upbeat. Steve was a family man, active in his church, a father, and an all-around nice guy.

Several months after being hired, one of my managers began to question Steve's integrity. She thought Steve was logging calls into our CRM system that he in fact never made. As I mentioned earlier, our BDMs are required to make a certain number of calls each day. She brought this to my attention and shared her reasoning and concern.

We decided to watch him a little closer to see if we could verify her concern. At the time, it was not easy to extract call logs from our phone system and then compare to what was logged into our CRM. After monitoring Steve for a few days, we decided to pull him in and share our concern.

The manager met with Steve and shared her concern. Steve denied the accusation. After the meeting, things seemed to change, and it was back to business as usual.

As we approached the end of the year, we implemented a large Sales contest in an effort to finish the year out strong. We set up five teams of BDMs. Each team had three BDMs, and one of them was the leader. Steve was the leader of his team.

The contest was designed to pay the winning team $5,000. The $5,000 was divided among the team members based on their results within the team. The team member with the highest results received $2,500, second place received $1,500, and third place received $1,000.

Steve's team won the $5,000. Steve was the highest on his team and walked away with a $2,500 bonus at Christmastime.

Shortly after the contest, there were once again grumblings that Steve was falsely logging calls and had been less than honest during the contest. I was faced with this in the past, I was faced with it now, and I knew I would be faced with it again in the future. As a result, I purchased call accounting software that interfaced with my phone system.

This new software would track actual dials made. I could then compare this to my CRM reports to see if they balanced. Sure enough, once I got the software up and running, Steve's numbers were not matching.

We once again pulled Steve in and confronted him. This time, he admitted to the charge.

Our employee handbook states that this can be grounds for termination. We explained to Steve that it could not continue and decided not to terminate his employment. We liked Steve. We thought he was a good guy that simply got caught up doing something he shouldn't be doing.

Wouldn't you know, three days later Steve was doing the same thing again. I pulled him into my office and told him his employment was terminated. I escorted Steve to his desk, stayed there while he cleaned out his personal belongings, and walked him to the door.

Later, I was told that Steve cheated during the contest, which helped him win. Others knew it, and as a result, Steve's actions tainted the entire contest. By not addressing the issue sooner, when I first knew it was a problem, I weakened the integrity of the organization. I should have made the tough decision at the moment I knew it was a problem.

It should have been addressed, and it wasn't. The problem was that everyone else knew that it was happening.

What did I learn? I learned that when you believe there is an issue, you should address it immediately. Don't allow it to brew and become a bigger problem. Maintain your integrity and your principles, and move on.

I have made serious investments to know what my BDMs are and are not doing. I have invested in a phone system that records their calls. We use this information as a training tool. We sit with each of our BDMs and dissect random calls and discuss how we can improve. These call recordings provide our managers with first-hand exposure to what our BDMs are doing and what they are saying. We have performance managers who are dedicated to working with the BDMs intimately each day. The performance manager's role was created to help us have accurate information regarding what our BDM staff is doing and not doing. The performance manager walks the floor all day, assisting, training, and reviewing every lead that is generated for quality purposes.

How close are your Sales managers to your Sales reps? How much do they really know what is going on? If you don't have a CRM effectively implemented within your group, how do you really know what your Sales reps are doing? How often are your Sales managers out in the field with your Sales reps? You may be saying that you cannot afford to have your Sales reps spend that much time with your Sales managers. But it will cost you much more to have Sales reps in the field that are not working, are ineffective, or are misrepresenting your company, products, and services.

Having KPIs and the means to measure daily, weekly, and monthly performance helps us make quicker and more informed decisions. Now, when we know that a BDM is not a good fit, we make the decision to move on quickly. We owe it to our company and to our customers to make the tough decisions.

Sales Managers need to be able to make the tough decisions when they need to be made. You need to have measuring sticks in place to monitor and to gauge if there is a potential problem before it becomes a problem.

Getting rid of poor performers sends a message to your group. It says that in order to work here, you need to perform at this level. It raises the standard. It instills a sense of pride. It makes them feel good that they work for a company that demands performance and that they are meeting that standard.

As the Sales manager, you should be the busiest Sales person in the company. You should be intimately involved in each of your Sales reps' business. You should have KPIs in place to measure and monitor. You should ensure that you have the most effective, most efficient Sales organization possible.

Is your Sales approach effective? Do you really have the best Sales reps? Do you have the right Sales manager?

Truth #5—Your Sales manager isn't doing all he or she can do.

CHAPTER 8

LET THE TRUTH BE TOLD

So what have we uncovered about the truth of Sales within your organization?

Many companies struggle because they have not clearly defined Sales. An unclear definition of Sales weakens the entire Sales process and structure. There must be a clear definition, and everyone must understand his or her role.

As result, we defined Sales in the following way:

> "Sales focuses on finding and closing new business
> from new customers 100 percent of the time."

If you are most like organizations, your Sales staff is spending very little time, if any, prospecting for new business. Prospecting for new business from new customers must be as important as any other part of your Sales process.

The moment you place that level of importance and emphasis on prospecting is the moment that you will begin to change things inside your Sales organization.

Our Concept states,

> "Finding and closing new business from new customers
> needs to be separated from all other Sales initiatives."

The only way to ensure that you will get 100 percent focus and dedication to prospecting for new business from new customers is to assign this task to a dedicated person or group. To do so, you must remove any other responsibilities. If not, you will never get the level of time and effort you need. Sales reps will always migrate to what they like the most or what is easiest. In either case, most will never migrate to cold calling and prospecting.

We also discussed the need to make changes. You have underachievers on your Sales team. This isn't a surprise; you have known this for quite a while but simply haven't addressed it. One of the reasons you haven't addressed it is because you aren't doing your job. Sales is the heartbeat of your organization. Having the right Sales people in the right positions is critical to your success.

Sales is the most mismanaged group within your organization. There are Sales reps working out of their homes, in which case we don't know what they are doing. We don't know whom they contacted today, this week, last week, or ever. We don't know if they are up and working by 8 a.m. We don't know if they are working till 5 p.m. They fool us by sending us an email using their Blackberry at 7 a.m. or 7 p.m. We would not manage any other group within our organization as loosely as we manage Sales. Our Sales group must be managed to the same level, if not higher, than our accounting department and operations. Remember, without Sales, we wouldn't need accounting and operations.

We must define specific KPIs to measure and monitor our Sales reps' activity levels. We live under a fallacy, believing there are no immediate consequences for poor Sales performance. There are immediate consequences, and we must be able to indentify problem areas as they happen. Having a strong CRM tool that is appropriately and efficiently used can be an effective Sales tactic.

Lastly, we may have the wrong Sales manager at the helm. The Sales manager needs to be an effective leader. He or she needs to demand performance and lead by example. It is his or her job to set the goals and the process to hit those goals. It is his or her job to ensure that the company employs productive and effective Sales reps. This is a good place to start. Make sure you have the right person steering your ship.

CHAPTER 9

CALL TO ACTION

I understand that I have made some very bold statements in this book. I realize that much of what I have stated may appear to be negative. I accept that not all organizations are as I described in the preceding pages. However, I am confident that many are exactly as I have described.

If your organization falls into this category, then take the first step by admitting it. Identifying that your Sales organization has serious shortcomings is the first step, and it is a big one. However, don't fool yourself that by simply admitting it that you are on the right track to successful change and positive results.

You have a call to action. When are you going to do to address these very critical areas of your Sales organization? There is no time to waste. The market, your customers, and your competition aren't waiting for you. They are moving forward.

I believe there are some very specific steps that need to be taken to get your Sales group on task. There may need to be a mindset change from how things were done in the past. The number-one hurdle I run into when working with our clients is overcoming their mindset that they have always done it this way in the past and, consequently, it is difficult for them to consider a new structure, a new methodology, and a new process. We must accept that how we sold five to ten years ago may not be the same as what is required today. I believe some things in Sales never change. However, other aspects of Sales require drastic change.

I encourage you to read *Concept, Process, and Discipline*, which is the follow-up to *Time For Change*. In that book, I provide a detailed approach on how to set up an effective Sales structure.

After reading either of these two books, I encourage you to contact me directly to discuss your specific needs and questions. Please feel free to contact me at dharsh@conceptservicesltd.com.

Thank you for taking the time to read *Time For Change*. I hope you were able to walk away with something that you can apply to your specific situation.

ABOUT THE AUTHOR

My career spans over thirty years. During this time, I have held the positions of inside Sales, outside Sales, Sales manager, vice president of Sales, and owner of two companies. I understand the Sales process and the mentality of the Sales rep. My career has always centered on Sales. I have done my share of cold-calling, appointments, speaking engagements, managing Sales reps and territories, designing and implementing CRM solutions, and more. The one thing that was always constant was my dislike of cold-calling. I loved to go on appointments and to be in front of the customer. However, I hated making the cold calls to get appointments. As a result, I formed Concept Services. If I hated to make cold calls, then I believed there were lots of Sales reps that hated to make cold calls. If this were true, then companies were struggling with gaining opportunities to get in front of new prospects and customers. I formed Concept Services to focus on the part of Sales that most people hate, and that is cold-calling. Over the years, Concept Services has become very proficient and effective in this role. We have developed a process and methodology that works. I believe that to be successful in anything, you must be disciplined. Concept Services is built on discipline.